MW00613164

PRAISE FOR *The Wild Jalopy*

"This is a love story. Two extraordinary people, two extraordinary intellects...joined in their love for each other, in their love of words, in their love for the art of life. Thoreau must be smiling as Kathleen's jalopy arrives, still whir-whirring, shot into the harmony of it all."

—DALE M. HERDER, PH.D., PROFESSOR OF ENGLISH AND VICE PRESIDENT EMERITUS

"This posthumously published collection of Kate Hopkins' poetry is a testament to her talent, a celebration of her unique place in the world, and a preservation of the wonder that she was to her loving husband, Howard."

—JILL REGLIN

"*The Wild Jalopy* is a wonderful collection of poems that skillfully evoke several of our more noble, and sometimes fragile, sentiments. It is a moving, elegant tribute to living, and to being human."

—TIM MIANK, RETIRED ENGLISH PROFESSOR

"There are times in life when only poetry will do. Luckily, for us, Kathleen Potemko Hopkins turned to poetry during a range of experiences over her lifetime. In *The Wild Jalopy*, Hopkins brilliantly distills her thoughts and emotions to capture her experience of national and international crises, interactions with her children, and moments of inner clarity. Through poems spanning her lifetime, she reveals astonishing intellectual and emotional depth—both in times of crisis and in moments of quiet reflection at the wonders of the natural world. In *The Wild Jalopy*, Hopkins reveals a life well-lived, and she will inspire you to do the same."

—KATHARINE MARVIN

"This is a book about generosity. The generosity of spirit that comes naturally to a few rare souls who we are lucky to know. One might think that gift came effortlessly to Kathleen Hopkins, but as you read these poems you see how she savored the journey on the wild ride of life, and the space and time that she traversed on the trek. Michael Morris' pen and ink illustrations add just the right complement to the meditations."

—GLENN WOLFF, ARTIST AND ILLUSTRATOR

"*The Wild Jalopy* is a brief and beautiful collection of poetry that is not only a celebration of a woman's body of work, but also a personal record of a man's admiration for the love of his life."

—JUAN PINEDA

The Wild Jalopy

Published by Mission Point Press
2554 Chandler Rd.
Traverse City, MI 49696
(231) 421-9513
www.MissionPointPress.com

Design by Sarah Meiers

ISBN 978-1-958363-73-7

Printed in the United States of America

Kathleen Potemko Hopkins

The
Wild
Jalopy

MISSION POINT PRESS

FOREWORD

"She was a phantom of delight."
—William Wordsworth

During the summer, my wife and I often sat together in the yard and watched the butterflies on our lilacs, putting us in mind of Wordsworth's "To a Butterfly." As the afternoons passed, we felt the summer together, as in Emily Dickinson's "The Bee is not afraid of me":

The Bee is not afraid of me.
I know the Butterfly.
The pretty people in the Woods
Receive me cordially—

The Brooks laugh louder when I come—
The Breezes madder play;
Wherefore mine eye thy silver mists,
Wherefore, Oh Summer's Day?

Kate had a giving spirit, a keen wit, and a creative mind. I always thought of her as a renaissance individual, someone who could do just about anything and do it perfectly. She was a quick study, which aided her intelligence. She did the research, then solved the problem.

She was far and away my intellectual superior, but because of her kindness of heart, she never intentionally made the difference apparent to me. I saw her intelligence in everything she did—in her poetry, in her art, in the level of her reading interests (especially physics), and in her music (she appreciated all genres). She loved her piano and derived much pleasure in having taught herself how to play. Writing, too, came to her naturally; she was so fluent.

Kate knew how to live her life—with high standards and sound ethics. How blessed was I to receive the benefits of her companionship. Was she a saint? Of course not. But to me, she was a wonder. She came into my life when I was less than I could be, and when she left my life, I was a whole person. What more could anyone ask of a wife?

Even as she struggled to fight an aggressive cancer through the last three months of her life, she remained aware of the needs of her family and others, identifying charities, making sure I would be alright. She kept making notes about what needed to be done. One note told me, "Whatever you do, don't give in to grief!"

And so it is with joy that I share this small collection of her poems.

Yes, my Kate, "love endures in my soul."

Howard

THE WILD JALOPY

Time's company is fading.
Gone the muscle-loose adolescent
Riding the wild jalopy.

Another being now.

Still stunned, stunned still,
Skin thinned, body blanched,
Reshaping time, contemplating circles.

I am still. I still am—

Riding the wild jalopy:
A habit of joy, a thing of itself,
Cash and carry,
       the doing,
       the trying,
       the moving,
       the whirr-whirr
       motor running,
       headlong fling flung
Gotta' go.

1997

ON READING

Touch my mind
                    with the stars
that wander above me
                    and beyond.
Let their fire linger to
                    ravage my calm
with that passion,
                    that silent swirling
wild into my mind.

This desire for what
                    I cannot see
stills the passing
                    of my days,
weaving, turning,
                    leaving patterns
burning, until I explode
                    into the universe,
shot into the harmony of it all.

January 20, 1997

Shelf Life

Breathe

SHELF LIFE

Inside my pen my soul waits
        to fly, to feel,
        to fold open on the page.
Cells of my soul blue-written,
        wild-wound, then formed,
        and re-formed,
Leaving this page of me
        torn free and still.

Still, adrift, season-shorn,
Undone, unseen, until you

Breathe me into your mind—
        this page,
        this flat-fashioned piece,
To wake, and wander, and wind
        through you;
        to crackle
Life-lit. Lifted free.

1997

LIKE A CHILD WONDER-WORN

This weight,
           my soul embedded in the past
           leadens,
           dusts and deadens every now
           like a penalty for living,
           hiding the free-flowing,
           flying, wild wonder
           of living lightly.

Come freedom,
           burning shadows dark to white
           and open me with passion
           to ignite each moment
           with particles of color
           showering bright into my soul
           a creative fire.

Then, leaning breathless into expectation,
           peering past time's limitation
           to see all that is—
           to be in it, and of it,
           around it and through,
           unfolding time
           enfolding every now,
           inside out with delight,

To rest, in placid satisfaction,
Like a child wonder-worn.

1997

THE MORNING AFTER

She stands at the edge of time as
Words of iron and ice and steel shot
Fall one then one then one, blunt,
Spent, and pile comfortably at her feet.

Before she leaves, she bends
To gather the load and puts them
Away in their usual place; and she
Puts them away in their usual place.

She sleeps and washes each word
With ignorance, until iron and ice and
Steel shot blur. Morning comes joined
To her like a sister, full of knowledge
And secret plans, and full of secret plans.

1998

ON THE NEWS AGAIN

What are they doing here in the Suburbs,
Those people in babushkas and tired shoes
Sprouting from mud into the showers—
Not polished brass on ceramic, preheated,
Clean, very clean, showers; but
Dropped-out-of-the-clouds-and-into
Their-faces and into-their-children's-faces
Rain, for God's sake.

Sagging, soggy, worn down people,
Fleeing, falling, wheeling Daddy's body
In a cart, and floating—

Floating on my new TV. Slapping me
From my entertainment center
In my brick and roughsawn mortgaged life
That I've worked my ass off for—
Kissing-up, career-path, business-casual work
With my business-casual spouse.

And now those Peacekeepers in camouflage
Had better go over there and fix it; so that
Those people in babushkas and tired shoes

Are not on the six o'clock news again.
Finally, an address where I can send a relief
Check. Thank God.

November 1999

ECLIPSED

In midnight clothes, bare feet,
I grasped the moon
With my eyes;
Cold slapping me clear
Into the night still.

All still.

Until a monolith loosed
From some seed, some speck
In me, unexpectedly lifting
Me out away, clean away,
Lifting me to the icy still.

I was nothing.

I was all. Rising in earth's
Boundless shadow falling,
Light-years lost, leaving land
And lying silent
On the moon. Still.

All still.

Into my skin a cement chill
Wriggled senses free from
Sky to ground, collapsing me.

A speck again telling, as
I shrink to fill my space—

I am here. I am here.

(*Watching the lunar eclipse of March 23, 1997*)

NAKED IF KIND

(a reflection on terror)

We're naked, if kind
To see with compassion
Soul for soul

And shot with sorrow's
Gentle hand.
Show me the way

Through the cold, the violent
Days, each alone. Gentle hand,
Show me the way.

September 11, 2001

FOR DANIEL

Fly he must,
       wings light,
             lifted
                      aloft on the
       thoughts of those
             with him.

Dear and stubborn heart
       trusts in seasons' time
             to return again.

*(Written on the occasion of Daniel's
move to Texas, April 4, 1996)*

POTTY TRAINING

"It's time," Lisa said.
"Uh, huh, Jack is ready."
"Not a problem," said Dan;
"I've made plans already."

"Let's start with a list."

"Hmmm, potty training," Dad mused.
"What will we need?"
"Lumber, of course, nails, paint,
And a motor and a fuse."

"My mission is this—

"Jack needs a place for his potty,
And a reason to choose it—
I'll build on an addition."
"Yeah, with surround-sound included."

Lisa gave him a kiss.

And so it was built: the new potty,
And the addition with stereo and all,
And Jack learned from Dad that
It's no problem:

Have a Plan, Make a List, and Give it
Your All.

By Kate Hopkins (Gramma), February 2002

CLOUDS

I see you hovering over city streets
        or dusting bronzed country land—

I imagine you laughing at our world,
        at our cares and battle plans.

When tired of your place in the sky,
        you perch upon the tail of a breeze;

And like a wandering gypsy man,
        you slide across the sky.

May 1964

EVENING ETUDE

Gently ease my skin,
Fair weather,
Winter's worn and
Turned his face,
But here, crickets
Swing the dusk-dulled,
Dampish end of day
Into song-frames sung
Trilling, rolling rhythm
Bound by the bass of
A courting amphibian.

1997

Afterword

"Some day my happy arms will hold you,
And some day I'll know that moment divine,
When all the things you are, are mine!"
    —"All the Things You Are,"
        sung by Ella Fitzgerald

I am now finding many of Kate's journals, journals she wrote in every night. They reveal her depth of soul and her range of mind. For me, they provide rich insight and speak to me about what is important in life.

For you, Kate,

I walk to find a lonely trail,
A grassy meadow, a deep dale,
Away from noise, people and hate,
A secret place to meditate,
Where in sylvan silence, I can mend
My heart and soul before the end.

With All My Love,
Howard

About the Author

Kathleen Hopkins was an extraordinary person who lived an ordinary life. She did not have a handful of degrees and professional achievements, but she did accomplish something all important: a life well lived. Kathleen was a person of keen intelligence and wide-ranging interests. A native Michigander, she was happiest in well-worn flannel, denim, and trekking boots, hiking on a backwoods trail or two-track. She was a lifelong student of nature, science, art, and design, and she personally designed and planted hundreds of native plant habitats. Kathleen earned a degree in computer science, which she used to do extensive and careful research. She was a gourmet cook of healthy dishes—with the occasional fat and juicy ballpark-style hot dog stuffed with smoked Gouda and Vidalia onion and wrapped in bacon. Self-taught, she was a pianist of everything from light-tripping sonatinas to growling blues and ragtime. Kathleen had a serious interest in matters of the intellect and, more importantly, matters of the heart: she was the steadfast head of her family. Endlessly kind and generous, Kathleen gave substantial support to the Cherryland Humane Society in Traverse City, Michigan, and established two scholarships at Northwestern Michigan College: one in Fine Arts and the other in Creative Writing. Having managed her cancer with her husband, Howard, until the very last day, she and Howard were together when she passed away in the peaceful setting of Munson Hospice House.